ART & FEAR

ART
&
FEAR

*Observations
On the Perils (and Rewards)
of Artmaking*

DAVID BAYLES
TED ORLAND

THE IMAGE  CONTINUUM

SANTA CRUZ, CA & EUGENE, OR

Book Design by Ted Orland
Special Thanks to Mary Ford for additional design help.

Library of Congress Cataloging-in-Publication Data

Bayles, David.

Art & Fear:
Observations on the Perils (and Rewards) of Artmaking

p.   cm.
ISBN 0-9614547-3-3 (previously ISBN 0-88496-379-9)

1. Artists – Psychology. 2. Creation (Literary, artistic, etc.)
3. Artist's block. 4. Fear of failure.

I. Orland, Ted   II. Title.   III. Title: Art & Fear.

N71.B37   1993   93-27513
701'.15 – dc20   CIP

Published by
IMAGE CONTINUUM PRESS
P.O. Box 5243, Santa Cruz CA 95062-5243

Distributed to the Trade by
Consortium Book Sales & Distribution, Inc.
1045 Westgate Drive, Suite 90, Saint Paul MN 55114

Capra Press Edition
Twelve printings, March 1994 – November 2000

IMAGE CONTINUUM PRESS EDITION
First Printing, January 2001
2nd Printing, August 2001

for Jon, Shannon & Ezra

CONTENTS

PART I

INTRODUCTION

THE NATURE OF THE PROBLEM   1
     A Few Assumptions

ART & FEAR   9
    Vision & Execution
     Imagination
      Materials
     Uncertainty

FEARS ABOUT YOURSELF   23
     Pretending
      Talent
     Perfection
     Annihilation
      Magic
    Expectations

FEARS ABOUT OTHERS   37
    Understanding
     Acceptance
     Approval

FINDING YOUR WORK   49
      Canon

CONTENTS

PART II

THE OUTSIDE WORLD   65
Ordinary Problems
Common Ground
Art Issues
Competition
Navigating the System

THE ACADEMIC WORLD   79
Faculty Issues
Student Issues
Books about Art

CONCEPTUAL WORLDS   93
Ideas and Technique
Craft
New Work
Creativity
Habits
Art & Science
Self-Reference
Metaphor

THE HUMAN VOICE   113
Questions
Constants
vox humana